A BRIEF HISTORY OF ENGLAND

TRACING THE CROSSROADS OF CULTURES AND CONFLICTS FROM THE CELTS TO THE MODERN ERA

DOMINIC HAYNES

© **Copyright - Dominic Haynes 2021 - All rights reserved.**

The content contained within this book may not be reproduced, duplicated or transmitted without direct written permission from the author or the publisher.

Under no circumstances will any blame or legal responsibility be held against the publisher, or author, for any damages, reparation, or monetary loss due to the information contained within this book. Either directly or indirectly. You are responsible for your own choices, actions, and results.

Legal Notice:

This book is copyright protected. This book is only for personal use. You cannot amend, distribute, sell, use, quote or paraphrase any part, or the content within this book, without the consent of the author or publisher.

Disclaimer Notice:

Please note the information contained within this document is for educational and entertainment purposes only. All effort has been executed to present accurate, up to date, and reliable, complete information. No warranties of any kind are declared or implied. Readers acknowledge that the author is not engaging in the rendering of legal, financial, medical or professional advice. The content within this book has been derived from various sources. Please consult a licensed professional before attempting any techniques outlined in this book.

By reading this document, the reader agrees that under no circumstances is the author responsible for any losses, direct or indirect, which are incurred as a result of the use of the information contained within this document, including, but not limited to, — errors, omissions, or inaccuracies.

CONTENTS

Introduction   5

1. Ancient Influences and Ancestors (c. 600 BCE to 1066 CE)   7
2. French Foreigners to Essential Englishmen (1066-1453)   17
3. Thorns and Roses (1455-1603)   25
4. A Roiling Crucible of Revolution and Reform (1603-1801)   33
5. The Empire's Ascendency and Apex (1801-1918)   43
6. Battles, Blood, and the Death of Imperialism (1914-Present Day)   49

Other books by Dominic Haynes   61
References   63

HOW TO GET A FREE HISTORY EBOOK

Would you like a free copy of a surprise history ebook?

Get free and unlimited access to the below surprise history ebook and all of my future books by joining my Fan Base.

Scan with your camera to join!

INTRODUCTION

Off mainland Europe's western coast lies a rugged island, beset by winds and rain, and encircled by iron-gray waters. Island nations can often develop in isolation, creating singular cultures that are not exposed to outsiders until much later in their evolution, but this is not the case for this particular island. Here, instead of fostering the growth of an insular civilization, this land became a crossroads for many different cultures and peoples over the years. It is home to the three countries of England, Scotland, and Wales and the cradle of English, the most widely spoken language of the modern era.

The stark white and red flag bearing St. George's Cross identifies one of the three countries that make up this island of Britain: England. So how does this small portion of an island end up carrying a role in world history that is far larger than the acreage the country actually occupies? How does its language become the world's dominant tongue? As the seat of one of the last monarchs in the world, England and its government has survived by adaptation to and adoption of the cultures it has come into contact with. How else could tea and chicken tikka masala, both Asian in origin and heritage, become two of the country's most enduring cultural and gastronomic staples? England has long been defined by the cultures that inhabited the land, influenced by the cultures it conquered, and shaped by the brutal and bloody conflicts that have burdened its people from its earliest days.

1

ANCIENT INFLUENCES AND ANCESTORS (C. 600 BCE TO 1066 CE)

Before the Romans, the Angles, the Saxons, the Jutes, the Vikings, and the Normans, there was another, an earlier inhabitant of England's shores. A loosely associated group of tribes that originated out of Central Europe known as the Celts proliferated across the continent and into the British Isles. The Celts in England, known mostly as Britons, spoke a Celtic language, Common Brittonic, which is similar to Welsh and Gaelic. Although there is evidence of an antecedent and indigenous agrarian culture during the Neolithic Period--they are thought to be the ancient peoples who erected Stonehenge--not much is known about these native inhabitants, though their ancestors were most likely absorbed over time into the Celtic culture as it spread through the island. Being an Iron Age civilization, the Britons brought the use of the iron plow to the land and cultivated distinctive rectangular fields that can still be viewed in the present day. Allegedly warlike and fearsome, much of what is known about the Britons comes from outside sources, like the Romans, who saw the Celtic tribes of Europe as a threat to be tamed. Though they are seen now as a unit, the Britons were a patchwork of various tribes, and it was their failure to unify that ultimately led to the Roman occupation of England, bringing an end to Celtic dominance in the area with their successful invasion under Emperor Claudius in 43 CE.

Known as Britannia by the Romans, the land had first been assaulted by Julius Caesar around 55 BCE, and was finally under Roman authority roughly one hundred years later. The Romans brought their language, legions, and laws to England while attempting to expand their control into Wales and Scotland, known by the Romans as Cambria and Caledonia, respectively. Although Roman legions managed to make some headway into Wales, it never underwent the same Romanization seen to the east. Scotland, on the other hand, was another matter entirely. The Romans had continued to press northward, fighting against the Celtic Caledonians until their defeat at the hands of Julius Agricola around 81 CE, but the Caledonians remained a thorn in the side of the Romans, continually menacing the northernmost reaches of the Roman Empire. Eventually, in 117 CE, Emperor Hadrian had a wall erected near the modern-day border between England and Scotland to control the movement of people into and out of the territory and to separate the Roman settlements from the perceived "barbarians." The Caledonians would remain a threat, continually attacking and breaching Hadrian's Wall whenever the Roman legions were called away to other troubled reaches of the empire. By the end of the Roman occupation, these people were referred to as the Picts and the Scots.

Around the time of the Roman invasion of England, a tribe of Britons known as Icenis in the eastern portion of the country (known later as East Anglia) was ruled by a fierce red-haired queen, Boudicca. After the death of her husband, her property was seized by Roman soldiers, her daughters were raped, and she was beaten in public while many of her Iceni people were enslaved. Enraged, she led the Iceni and several other Celtic tribes into rebellion, sacking London and St. Albans (known then as Londinium and Verulamium). Eventually, the Romans defeated the Britons, and Boudicca is rumored to have taken her own life to avoid Roman captivity.

After suppressing Boudicca and her followers, England under the Romans was relatively peaceful, and the infrastructure they laid down had a lasting impact on how the country would be built and settled well into the future. The towns of York, Bath, and Lincoln were all founded under Roman rule, and the many military roads they built to connect these cities to the harbor in London remain linked by their system to this day. England benefited economically from the sheer vastness of the Roman Empire, allowing them to trade with a larger audience and come into contact with luxury goods from distant lands. Though the Romans had invaded the country and still maintained a heavy military presence to ward off the outlying Celtic tribes, they did not supplant the local population. Rather, the upper classes that had been present before the Roman invasion simply adopted Roman ways of living, dressing, and speaking, while the lower classes continued to operate as they always had, scraping out a living from the land beneath their feet.

Eventually, as Rome rotted away from within, their hold on Britain waned. Caledonians continually chipped away at the northern border, while tribes of Saxons from Central Germany, initially brought to the island to help fend off invaders from Scotland and Ireland, began to pillage along the southern and eastern coastline of Britain. By the time the western half of the

Roman Empire finally crumbled in 476 CE, the Romanized Britons had been on their own for some time and had already fallen under the influence of the new Anglo-Saxon invaders. Rome had connected the British Isles to the rest of mainland Europe through commerce and trade, and this relationship would continue to be crucial to the future of the island nation of England. The Romans had also brought Latin with them, one of the most influential ancestors of the English language. But aside from the ruins left behind and the roads they built, Rome left England with a religion that would shape society for centuries to come. As Roman influence shrank away, Christianity remained an enduring institution.

Central and Western Germanic tribes known as the Angles, Saxons, Jutes, and Frisians had been used by the Roman Empire to defend Britannia from the Caledonians and Irish tribes, but now with the legions gone, these same tribes were settling in England. Regarded by the Romano-British population as outsiders, and resisted by Celtic tribes in Wales and Scotland, the Germanic tribes were initially met with hostility. Around this time, the legend of King Arthur is set, with Arthur as a Romano-Briton leader resisting the new interlopers. However, these were bellicose people, and the Romanized and defenseless Britons did not pose much of a challenge. It should be noted that very little written record survives from this time, so it cannot be said definitively how much violence the Angles and Saxons enacted on the Britons versus how much the Britons simply allowed themselves to be absorbed into the new culture, much as they had with the Romans before them. Either way, as the Anglo-Saxon people spread, they brought the Old English language to England, to which the Germanic base of modern English is owed. Their monarchical system of government paired with a kind of proto-parliament known as the Witan laid the groundwork for the country's present-day Parliament and constitutional monarchy. Furthermore, many names of cities and regions in England owe their names to the Anglo-Saxons. To wit, though the Romans had called the area Britannia, it soon gained the name "Land of the Angles" which in time was simplified into England.

By 650 CE, seven Anglo-Saxon kingdoms had been established: Essex, Sussex, Wessex, East Anglia, Mercia, Northumbria, and Kent. Over the next two hundred years, the seven kingdoms would merge into three-- Wessex, Mercia, and Northumbria--with Mercia being the largest and most influential prior to the 800s CE. Though Mercia enjoyed the largest landmass and had historically been the more politically powerful kingdom, the royal Windsor family of the twenty-first century does not trace its lineage back to the ancient monarchs of Mercia. That honor is possessed by the rulers of Wessex. When the powerful King Ecbert of Wessex came to power in the early 800s CE, he subdued Mercia and set the stage for the unification of Mercia and Wessex under his grandson, Alfred the Great, known as King of the English. The final fusion of Wessex, Mercia, and Northumbria into England was achieved under the first King of England and Ecbert's great-great-grandson, Aethelstan.

While Anglo-Saxon society started to establish itself, stabilize, and flourish in the 700s CE, a new wave of marauding trespassers began to eye the growing wealth. Natives of Scandinavia, known by the Anglo-Saxons as the Danes, the Norse, or the Northmen, Vikings descended on the British Isles in the late 700s CE. Beginning with initial raiding and pillaging, by the reign of Alfred the Great in the 800s, these attacks had turned into permanent settlements. After multiple bitter clashes with Viking forces, Alfred withdrew to the Somerset Marshes to regroup before successfully defeating the Vikings at the Battle of Edington in 878 CE. Alfred wisely realized that the Viking settlements were too entrenched and his own resources too depleted to fully remove them from England, so he negotiated a treaty with their king, Guthrum. This created a special territory in a portion of Northern and Eastern England known as the Danelaw, so the Viking settlers could live peaceably alongside the Anglo-Saxons.

Unfortunately, this hardly stopped the Viking threat, and the raiding and violence continued well into the ninth century. England would even have four Scandinavian monarchs after Sweyn Forkbeard seized the throne from his contemporary Saxon ruler, Aethelred II the Unready. The most successful of these four foreign sovereigns would be King Cnut, who ruled a vast empire that included England, Denmark, Norway, and a portion of Sweden. This realm was short-lived since his sons, Harthacnut and Harold were unable to control his North Sea Empire after his death. The English throne was reclaimed by Harthacnut's Saxon half-brother and Aethelred II the Unready's son, Edward the Confessor.

Though the Angl0-Saxon line was restored on the throne, Edward had spent the majority of his life in exile across the English Channel in Normandy. He had few allies in England, and needed the support of the noblemen, particularly his future wife's family, the Godwins, to secure his rule. When Edward died childless in 1066 CE, three tenuous claims to the English throne existed, throwing the nation into turmoil and chaos. The first was Harold Godwinson, who, though he had no royal blood, was the brother-in-law of the late king and brother to the queen. The second was Edgar Aetheling, the late king's great-nephew with the strongest blood claim, but little to no political capital to back it up. The third was William, the Duke of Normandy and cousin to the late king; his royal blood made him a strong contender, but his status as a foreigner made his claim questionable and somewhat unappealing.

2

FRENCH FOREIGNERS TO ESSENTIAL ENGLISHMEN (1066-1453)

In England, Harold claimed that Edward the Confessor had designated him to be the rightful heir to the throne, and well aware of the manifold claims to the crown, he had himself quickly enthroned. Following this, two forces began to amass and move towards England. The first was led by Harold's exiled brother Tostig and the King of Norway, Harold Hardrada, keen to gain power in England. The second was William, Duke of Normandy, enraged by Harold's claim to the throne. William's family had sheltered Edward the Confessor during his time of exile in Normandy and claimed that Edward had named William, not Harold as his successor many years before his death. So now the freshly minted King Harold of

England rode north to meet his brother's forces as William of Normandy prepared his troops.

King Harold was victorious over the combined armies of Tostig and Harold Hardrada at Stamford Bridge, but a few short weeks later when he rode south to meet the Normans, the tides had turned. Meeting on a field outside the town of Hastings, Harold and William's forces ferociously clashed. Harold died on the battlefield and in October of 1066, victorious in the Battle of Hastings, William of Normandy became William the Conqueror, the first Norman king of England.

Once again, a new culture and language began to sweep through England. The Normans were French-speaking Christians with Frankish and Scandinavian ancestry. By 1072, the Normans had their hands on the levers of power, supplanting the Anglo-Saxon nobles and government officials with their own appointees. The new ruling class of England spoke French, and for many years after, the monarchs of England rarely spoke English. For this reason, many words in the English language pertaining to the law and the government, like liberty, justice, and people, have French origins. Additionally, the idea of primogeniture--that the first-born son would inherit the crown--was imported with the Norman invasion. Under Anglo-Saxon rule, though it was common for the first-born son to be the next king, it was not guaranteed. The Witan controlled succession to the throne, electing a king from eligible candidates of royal blood.

The Normans brought architectural ideas from mainland Europe into the island, replacing old Saxon structures of wood with soaring gothic cathedrals made of stone. The impressive castles, cathedrals, and monasteries that dot the landscape of England are a result of the imported Norman aesthetics. William himself was highly organized, commissioning a massive survey 1085 to properly assess the wealth of his kingdom. The resulting documents were compiled into Domesday Book, which gives the reader an incredible look at how the land was divided and used, who owned what, and how disputes were settled.

When William died, he divided his lands between his sons, but his youngest son, Henry I would reunite Normandy and England under his rule by 1106. However, Henry I's son and heir would die in a drunken boat accident in the English Channel, paving the way for his daughter Matilda and her second husband, Geoffrey Plantagenet to lay claim to the English throne.

THE RISE OF THE PLANTAGENETS

Despite Matilda and Geoffrey's best efforts, the pair never ruled officially as Queen and King of England. It was instead, their son, Henry II who ascended to the throne with his queen, Eleanor of Aquitaine, and officially founded the Plantagenet Dynasty, ruling over all of England as well as a massive swath of France. The Plantagenets, also known as the Angevins due to their homeland of Anjou, were French in origin, and much like the Norman kings before them, spoke mostly French in their early days. These familial roots and claims to large portions of France would be the seeds for the seemingly never-ending struggle between the English and French monarchs for power in the region, as well as the source for the centuries-long bitter rivalry between the nations.

The Plantagenets were a ruthless and bloody family, frequently turning on one another when the circumstances suited them. Husband would turn against wife, brother against brother, and even father against son. The Angevin Kingdom's borders were ever-changing, with the often villainized King John, son of Henry II, losing the majority of French territory. After his failures abroad, John began to levy high taxes on the English nobles to ease the exhausted Royal Treasury. In response, with encouragement from the Archbishop of

Canterbury, the powerful barons rebelled in 1215, demanding an end to the abuses of royal power. John, outnumbered by the nobles, had no choice but to concede to their demands, leading to the signing of the Magna Carta in June of the same year. The Magna Carta laid out the rights the barons were owed, as well as guaranteeing the freedom of the Church, effectively neutering the possibility of an absolutist monarchy in England. Though the Magna Carta was not upheld in the short term, in the long run, it laid the foundation for the Constitution of England and foreshadowed the low tolerance the English would have for tyrannical monarchs in the future.

In addition to disagreements across the Channel with France, England began to assert its dominance over the entirety of the island. King Edward I the Longshanks brought Wales under English control with the Statute of Wales in 1284, and when his first son, also Edward, was born in Wales, Edward I proudly named his son Prince of Wales, a title that is held by the first-born son of the monarch of England to the present day. When Scotland had a succession crisis, Edward I seized the opportunity and began a long campaign to bring Scotland under his rule. For his brutal campaigns in the north, Edward I also earned the moniker "The Hammer of the Scots." However, Edward I and his son never managed to bring Scotland into the fold, and the nation would remain beyond England's grasp until the Stuart monarchs in the fifteenth century.

Back across the wind-whipped waters separating England and France, the King of France, Charles IV died without an heir in 1328, and King Edward III of England laid claim to the French throne since his mother had been Charles IV's sister. Edward III's forces arrived in France in 1339, commencing a long and brutal struggle between the two countries known as the Hundred Years' War (1337-1453). Initially, Edward III had resounding successes, with his forces and the forces of his son, The Black Prince, earning victory at the Battles of Crécy (1346) and Poitiers (1356) respectively. Over the next twenty years, the French began to push back, and by the Treaty of Bruges in 1375, many of Edward III's conquests evaporated, leaving England with the port of Calais and a small ribbon of coastline in Southern France. His losses in France led to disapproval at home, and the Bubonic Plague stalked the land, decimating the populace and sparking social and economic hardship.

Dissatisfaction among the peasant class continued to build after Edward III's death until an open rebellion broke out in 1381. A fourteen-year-old King Richard II rode out to meet the peasants, promising reforms that were never enacted. In contrast, Richard II became a highly authoritarian ruler with capricious tendencies, ultimately leading to his deposition at the hands of his cousin, Henry of Bolingbroke. Now crowned Henry IV, and the first English monarch to speak English as his foremost language, the Plantagenet line was beginning to drift from their French roots, seeing themselves more as Englishmen with ties and claims to the French throne, rather than Frenchmen who happened to occupy England. It was, in fact, Henry IV's son, Henry V, who made Chancery Standard English (Middle English) the official language of the government, and all records which had previously been in Latin or French were henceforth inscribed in English.

Henry V, like Edward III, laid claim to the French throne and continued the Hundred Years' War with France. At the Battle of Agincourt in 1415, Henry V defeated the French forces and continued on to gain territory in Normandy. Five years later, under the Treaty of Troyes (1420), Henry V was named heir to the throne of France and given the French King's daughter Catherine in marriage. Dying young from dysentery, his son, Henry VI was crowned the King of England in 1429 and King of France in 1431 following the death of his grandfather.

However, this English claim was hotly contested, especially by the former French King's son, the Dauphin. As the Dauphin went on to have multiple military successes against English forces in France, it was becoming clear that England could not hold France without it taking a massive toll on the country, and in 1453, the English withdrew to Calais. After some four hundred years of territorial disputes from William the Conqueror to King Henry VI, England ended up retaining only the port of Calais which would later be lost as well. The enmity between the nations and their respective monarchs did not dissipate, but the constant military campaigns momentarily subsided.

The Normans and Plantagenets had entered England as foreign monarchs, speaking French and imposing their customs and traditions on an Anglo-Saxon kingdom. However, a vibrant cultural exchange had taken place, and the formerly alien sovereigns saw themselves as distinctly English and separate from their habitual French enemies. The English language was spoken widely by both common and ruling classes, Geoffrey Chaucer was the leading literary voice of the day, and the previously exotic architectural style imported from mainland Europe created castles and cathedrals throughout England seen today as some of the nation's greatest cultural treasures.

3

THORNS AND ROSES (1455-1603)

Conflict abroad may have eased for the time being, but domestically, affairs were approaching a boiling point. The Plantagenets had always quarreled with one another for control over the various parts of their empire, and two particular branches of the family--the Lancasters and the Yorks--disagreed over who was the rightful occupier of the English throne. The current ruler, Henry VI was a Lancastrian as well as a feeble and ineffective king, seen as a danger to the kingdom by many, particularly Richard, Duke of York, a descendant of King Edward III with a claim to the English throne. The War of the Roses, a bloody civil war, broke out, and though the Duke of York was killed in battle, Richard's son Edward continued his cause, eventually defeating the Lancastrian forces in 1461. Claiming the crown for himself as Henry VI and his wife fled to Scotland, Edward IV became the first Yorkist king.

Power continually shifted between Lancastrian and Yorkist forces with both Henry VI and Edward IV occupying the throne at differing intervals, and the war dragged on for another thirty years. Eventually, savvy political maneuvering on the part of two women, Elizabeth Woodville and Lady Margaret Beaufort brought a young Henry Tudor to the throne in England, ending the War of the Roses. Lady Margaret Beaufort, though a minor noble, was related to the Lancaster family, and saw a way to put the crown on her son, Henry Tudor. By promising that her son would marry Elizabeth of York, Edward IV and Elizabeth Woodville's daughter, the Houses of Lancaster and York would be united on the throne of England. Summoned back from hiding in France, Henry Tudor landed surreptitiously in Wales, marching his forces northeast to Bosworth Field, where the allegedly unpopular current Yorkist King Richard III met his end in 1485.

THE TUDOR ROSE

Installed as King Henry VII, he immediately set about securing his legacy with his Yorkist wife, Elizabeth. A new coat of arms for the new dynasty represented the unification of the rival house, with the white rose of York superimposed over the red rose of Lancaster, creating the iconic Tudor Rose. He plastered this everywhere throughout the kingdom, and it can still be seen at the stunning chapel he added to Westminster Abbey (Henry VII Lady Chapel). Due to the unorthodox beginning of his rule, he found himself always fearful that he could be deposed, and though Henry VII was deeply shrewd and suspicious, it made him financially and diplomatically savvy. Upon his death in 1509, the treasury was full and he had locked his children into advantageous marriages. He had secured an alliance with Spain: first through the marriage of his son Arthur and later through his second son, Henry, to Katherine of Aragon, the daughter of King Ferdinand and Queen Isabella of Spain. One of his daughters was married to King James VI of Scotland, and the other was sent off to King Louis IX of France.

When Henry VII's first-born son Arthur died before he could ascend to the throne, both Arthur's bride and crown fell to the charming and charismatic Henry VIII. Deeply popular, well-educated, and seen as the Tudor Rose incarnate, Henry VIII's reign was much anticipated throughout the realm. Initially an ardent Catholic and dubbed a "Defender of the Faith " by the Pope, Henry VIII wrote the brilliant treatise, *Assertio Septem Sacramentorum* (*Defence of the Seven Sacraments*) in response to Protestant attacks on Papal authority by Martin Luther.

Young and hotheaded, Henry VIII had been intent on war with France to earn glory as Henry V had on the fields of Agincourt. But when early attempts failed, Henry VIII instead was persuaded by his advisors to avoid conflict with France and become the great peacemaker in Europe, signing the Treaty of Universal Peace with France. At the Field of the Cloth of Gold in 1520, King Henry VIII and King Francis I of France held a massive celebration of tournaments and feasting to show off their new friendship. Henry VIII's young daughter Mary was even betrothed to Francis I's son, the Dauphin for some time.

Within the British Isles, Henry VIII was also the first English king to be recognized as the King of Ireland, establishing control over the neighboring island with the Crown Act of 1542. This united the two nations, declaring that whoever was the monarch of England would also be the rightful monarch of Ireland.

However bright his early days, gray clouds of turmoil would soon fall over England. Much like his father before him, Henry VIII was intent on securing his legacy and his dynasty through a male heir, and only one of his daughters had survived. Katherine, his queen, tragically suffered the loss of five of her children--two stillborn daughters, a stillborn son, and two sons who did not live past infancy. This hunger for a male heir in combination with Henry VIII's infatuation with Lady Anne Boleyn set him on a collision course with the Pope in Rome and forever changed how England saw itself in the world.

Searching for a way to free himself from his marriage to Katherine of Aragon, Henry VIII claimed that since she had previously been wed to his brother, God had cursed their marriage, precluding them from producing living sons. When the Pope refused to grant Henry VIII an annulment, he broke with the Roman Catholic Church and set himself up as the head of the Church of England. Declaring that Popish authority over the country was not in England's best interests, Henry VIII managed to use a burgeoning sense of English identity and patriotism, as well as a looming threat of violence against those who protested, to grant his wishes. His marriage to Katherine was declared null and void, their daughter Mary was called a bastard, and Henry VIII wed Anne Boleyn, crowning her the new Queen of England.

Henry VIII's marriage to Anne would not produce a son either, but a daughter christened Elizabeth. He would finally get his son, Edward, with his third wife, Jane Seymour. Aside from his notorious marital record,

Henry VIII's break with the Catholic Church forever changed how England related to their monarch since the Head of the Church and the Head of the State were now bound up in one person. The Pope had long been the most powerful man in Europe, but Henry VIII sought to place himself at the same height. His challenge to Papal authority shook off the grip of religious fear Rome had held over the rulers of Europe for centuries and proved that kings could no longer be held in check by the Pope. He was a bold, proud, and audacious leader who left his mark on the English people and helped to establish a clear English identity on the world stage. However, his greatest legacy was bound up in his brilliant red-haired daughter, Elizabeth.

THE VIRGIN QUEEN

Shortly after Henry VIII's death, each of his three children occupied the throne in quick succession. First, his son Edward VI spent much of his short, youthful reign controlled by his advisors and powerful nobles. After his untimely death, his half-sister and daughter of Katherine of Aragon, Mary took the throne. Known eventually as Bloody Mary, she worked tirelessly to return England to the Catholic Church, and her means were often violent and ruthless. Upon her death in 1558, Elizabeth, daughter of Henry VIII and Anne

Boleyn, was crowned the Queen of England and proceeded to rule for an impressive forty-five years.

After the tumultuous tussles between Catholic and Protestant forces under her father and her siblings, Elizabeth I established peace between the faiths with the Thirty-Nine Articles in 1563; this likely spared her realm from further violence and bloodshed experienced throughout Europe at this time due to religious differences. As England stabilized under Elizabeth I, the country began to prove its mettle against the superpowers of Spain and France, sending voyagers like Sir Francis Drake out to explore new areas of the world. Elizabeth I recognized that an expansionary era of trade and colonization was on the horizon, and established the East India Trading Company near the end of her reign to ensure England's place among the great nations of the ensuing century.

Other nations in Europe began to take notice of the tiny island's potential, with the main power of the day, Catholic Spain, testing Elizabeth I in 1588. Spain, seeing England as a present religious threat and a future economic threat, sent a large armada north intending to gather the Spanish Army from the Netherlands to invade England. As the Spanish ships made their way into the English Channel and attempted to contact their army, the English navy mounted a fierce attack, and the invasion of England never came to fruition. However, the English naval resistance was not the main reason the Spanish Armada was unsuccessful. The Spanish Army was attacked, making the rendezvous with the armada quite difficult, the leader of the armada was inexperienced, and finally, the weather was rough and the winds were high, blowing the Spanish ships north and off course. Yet, Spain's failure had a positive effect on England both at home and abroad. The island nation had managed to repulse a major empire, and many English saw the weather's intervention as a sign that God was on their side. As a commemorative medal from the time read, "God blew and they were scattered."

Under Elizabeth I, the country certainly experienced a Golden Age of peace, prosperity, and a flourishing culture. One of the most abiding contributions of the Elizabethan Era was the work of William Shakespeare. A brilliant writer who reshaped the theatrical and literary spheres of the English language and whose work is still widely performed, adapted and read across the world today.

4

A ROILING CRUCIBLE OF REVOLUTION AND REFORM (1603-1801)

With Elizabeth I's death in 1603, Henry VII and Henry VIII's worst fears were realized; the Tudor dynasty had no direct heir, and the closest royal relative lay to the north in the royal Stuart family of Scotland. King James VI of Scotland was the son of Mary, Queen of Scots, and the great-great-grandson of Henry VII. Moving excitedly south, James VI of Scotland became James I of England. For the first time, the crowns of England and Scotland were united under one monarch, but Scotland retained their own parliament, as well as separate religious, educational, and legal systems. Though the son of an ardent Catholic and raised as a Presbyterian, James I operated under mostly Anglican tendencies throughout his reign, even attempting to bring the Church of Scotland under the same standards as the Church of England with the Articles of Perth in 1618.

Although there were several Catholic plots to replace Elizabeth I with her Catholic cousin and James I's mother, Mary, Queen of Scots, religious differences greatly deepened for much of the Stuart family's royal tenure. The tenuous peace Elizabeth I had achieved through her laissez-faire attitude towards religion was crumbling across the country. The famed and foiled Gunpowder Plot--a Catholic attempt to blow up Parliament, King James I, and his heir--early in his reign, led to an uptick in anti-Catholic sentiment and a government crackdown against any remaining Catholics in the country. Additionally, a faction of people, Puritans, who wished to purge the Church of England of any Roman-Catholic influences, traditions, and rites were growing in number and influence throughout Parliament.

With Catholic plots on one side and Puritan demands on the other, James I relied on his divine right to rule in order to keep the peace in his realm. James I had long ascribed to absolutist tendencies and had even penned an essay outlining his beliefs about the office of the king, *The True Law of Free Monarchies*. Absolute monarchies were de rigueur throughout Europe at this time, with James I's contemporaries in France, Spain, and

Russia all enjoying absolute power and authority over the nation. His predecessors, the Tudors had also been absolutist monarchs but had wisely kept Parliament involved, even if only nominally. After clashes over royal finances several years into his rule, and with James I firmly believing himself to be divinely right in all matters, it was no wonder that Parliament and the king rarely saw eye-to-eye. James I would frequently dissolve Parliament, only calling them back into session when fiscal matters or foreign relations necessitated it. Parliament, having been in session since 1604, was first dissolved by James I in 1611, and subsequently called back and dissolved in 1614, 1621, and 1624.

While the Thirty Years' War (1618-1648), a conflict fueled mainly by religious differences, raged on the continent of Europe, England found itself continually embroiled in domestic religious discord. James I's son, Charles I had come to the throne and though he professed the Anglican faith, he had married a Catholic woman and seemed to enjoy the more traditional and Catholic aspects of the rites and rituals in the Church of England. Public sentiment, especially in Parliament, was more in favor of the plainer, Puritan forms of worship that had continually gained traction since Henry VIII's break with Rome roughly a century earlier. Charles I continued his father's tradition of summoning and disbanding Parliament on a whim, ruling for eleven years straight at one point without once calling Parliament into session.

In 1641, spurred by an uprising in Ireland, Charles I was forced to recall Parliament to raise funds for an army. Parliament, wary of Charles I and unwilling to grant him the power of an army, declared that the troops could only be commanded by Parliament-approved officers. Charles I, in turn, simply called for all loyal citizens to join his army, and Parliament, now in alliance with Scottish Presbyterians, formed their own forces in response. Tensions between Parliament and the King continued to mount until it exploded into armed combat with the First English Civil War (1642-1646). Parliament's New Model Army, led by Oliver Cromwell, was far more disciplined and effective than the Royalist forces and decisive victories at Naseby (1644) and Marston Moor (1645) coupled with Charles I's attempts to gain military aid against his own people from abroad pushed public opinion away from the Royalist cause. Realizing his unfavorable position, Charles I surrendered himself to the Scottish Army, hoping to negotiate a deal in his favor.

Unfortunately for Charles I, he was handed over to the English Parliamentarians by the Scottish Army, and imprisoned on the Isle of Wight. Eventually in his captivity, Charles I managed to convince a faction of

Presbyterian Scots to defect to his cause with promises to support Presbyterianism in England upon his restoration to the throne. This ignited the Second English Civil War (1648) which was won by Cromwell and his New Model Army at the Battle of Preston. Determined by Parliament to be too dangerous if kept alive, King Charles I was charged with treason and executed in January of 1649. For the first time in its history, England was without a monarch, and Parliament took full control of the levers of power, abolishing the office of the king in February of the same year.

In the interluding decade before Charles I's son, Charles II was reinstated as the king, Oliver Cromwell, a member of Parliament and leader of the New Model Army, became Lord Protector of the Realm. Though Cromwell was now king in all but name, the ramifications of the English Civil War were clear; the ruler of England would have to listen to the people and the Parliament, or it could cost him his head. Absolutism and the divine right of kings were entering their waning days in England.

Crowned as King of Scotland three years after the execution of his father, Charles II was forced to flee to France when Cromwell and his forces managed to invade Scotland and proclaim the nations of England

and Scotland to be a unified commonwealth. In reality, this unification would not be a political actuality for another fifty years or so, with the Acts of Union in 1707 under Queen Anne. General unrest in Cromwell's England as well as the declining popularity of his policies resulted in the Stuart family's, particularly Charles II, restoration to power two years after Cromwell's death in 1658. After Charles II, the next in line to the throne was his Catholic brother, James II. England, being firmly Protestant at this juncture, was incredibly suspicious of this new Catholic ruler, and when his second wife, also a Catholic, gave birth to a son, fears of a stable and substantial Catholic Stuart dynasty prompted Protestants to begin searching for a suitable alternative.

A Dutch prince seemed like an odd choice for a monarch of England, but it would not be the first or the last time that a foreign power would sit on the English throne. William of Orange was married to James II's daughter Mary, a product of his first marriage, but most importantly, the pair were Protestant, not Catholic. Essentially invited to invade England, William of Orange landed with his forces in 1688, and many of James II's forces defected to William of Orange's cause. James II stole away to France, never again to sit on the throne. Meanwhile, William of Orange and his wife Mary were crowned by Parliament as joint rulers, becoming William III and Mary II. Thankful to now be rid of the absolutist Stuarts, Parliament seized the opportunity to gain the political upper hand over the Crown. They drew up a Declaration of Rights that set up a royal code of conduct, limited the power of the monarchy, made the monarchy reliant on Parliament for finances, and gave Parliament control of taxation and legislation. William III and Mary II accepted the terms, and the Glorious Revolution of 1688 established England as a constitutional monarchy.

It was not long until another succession crisis befell England. When William III and Mary II died childlessly, the throne fell to Mary II's younger sister, Anne. Yet Anne, though pregnant a devastating seventeen times, had only managed to have one surviving son who died at eleven years old. By contrast in France, James II's line had continued, and his son James Stuart was the closest relative and seemed likely to seize the throne upon Anne's death. However, Parliament, unwilling to have a Catholic return as the king, had passed the Act of Settlement in 1701 just before William III's death. This not only further restricted the power of the monarchy and cemented parliamentary supremacy, but it also forbade the accession of a Catholic to the throne of England. As a result, Parliament, knowing that the line of succession would be a thorny issue upon Queen Anne's death, began to search for an appropriate heir.

HANOVERIANS ARRIVE FROM GERMANY

In Hanover, Germany, Parliament found their answer. Princess Sophia, the well-educated and articulate Electress of Hanover, was the granddaughter of James I, and a Protestant. With both the right blood and religious pedigree, it was agreed that she would take the throne once Anne passed. Unfortunately, Sophia died before she could take the throne, and it was her less popular son, George, who arrived in her stead to establish the Hanoverian line in England in 1714. With many believing him to be unworthy of the crown, only one year into his rule, George I faced an uprising from the Scottish clans in support of James Stuart. Though English forces eventually took the day, it would not be the last armed conflict between the Scottish and the English over the legitimacy of the Stuart claim.

Speaking little English, George I was not a terribly well-liked king and was seen very much as an outsider. He relied heavily on his ministers to govern and spent much of his time away at his properties in Germany. Due to George I's more reticent approach to governance, the first Prime Minister, Robert Walpole largely maintained control of the country. By now the Parliament had already begun to divide into two political parties: the Whigs and the Tories. Though Parliament was largely controlled by the Whigs, Tories were still a present force, and they (either secretly or overtly) supported the Stuart claim to the throne. This unrest and general dissatisfaction with the Hanoverian kings continued during George I's son, George II's reign. The grandson of James II, Charles Stuart, "Bonnie Prince Charlie," like his father before him, had gathered the support of the Scottish clans and mounted the Jacobite Rebellion against King George II. In 1746, at the Battle of Culloden, the Jacobites were crushed and Scotland was forcefully subdued. Any further plots to challenge the Hanoverians had very little probability of success.

However, despite Hanoverian unpopularity, many wealthy Englishmen found themselves copying the fashion tastes of their new monarchs, especially a new style of architecture. This style, called Georgian, Neo-Palladian, or Neo-Classical is a revival of ancient Greek and Roman styles, recognizable by its colonnades, symmetrical and unadorned exteriors, and cavernous, sparsely decorated interiors. This was seen everywhere at the time, even in British colonies overseas. To this day, the style has remained particularly popular in government and university buildings in the United States, which would have been a major English colony under the early Hanoverian monarchs.

This fascination with Greek and Roman architecture is also explained by the ascendancy the British Empire was beginning to experience. England saw itself as the natural successor to the Roman Empire that had collapsed and receded from the shores of Britain so many ages before. With colonies across the world, an increasingly superior military force, and a growing dominance within the British Isles, England was developing quickly into a superpower while rival Spanish and French powers began to experience a decline. After a humiliating defeat for France and the hands of Great Britain during the Seven Years' War (1756-1763), England's colonial possessions and power, especially in the North American hemisphere, swelled. Though the American Colonies were lost in the American Revolution (1775-1783) shortly after this masterful moment of British dominance, and the economy was slightly dampened as a result, the glaring reality was that England was transforming into an empire on the rise. After the union between Britain (England, Scotland, and Wales) and Ireland established in 1801 and a census count of nine million souls, England was seen as a potentially dominant European power, placing it on a collision course with its old rival across the Channel once more. The English were not the only nation who believed their nation to be true Roman successors; the French had risen from the gore of their revolution and selected the First Consul of France, Napoleon Bonaparte.

5

THE EMPIRE'S ASCENDENCY AND APEX (1801-1918)

On the continent, France had become the dominant European power since its victory in the Thirty Years' War (1618-1648), unseating Spain and enjoying European supremacy for the next two hundred years or so. France had faced its internal obstacles to be sure, but in 1799, an ambitious and brilliant leader named Napoleon Bonaparte rose to power in the wake of the French Revolution. Initially styling France as a republic and calling himself the First Consul, it only took five short years before he began calling himself the Emperor of France, and an official coronation was held in 1804 at Notre Dame Cathedral.

Napoleon embarked on a brutal campaign, seizing much of Europe's landmass and embroiling the majority of the continental powers in the Napoleonic

Wars (1803-1815). Great Britain, an empire on the rise, was a clear military and economic threat to Napoleon's expansionary desires. Three years into the Napoleonic Wars, he enacted an economic blockade on Great Britain known as the Continental System, making trade and commerce incredibly difficult, though not all European powers were fully willing to comply with his scheme. England's old ally, Portugal, continually resisted. Beyond causing economic pain for England, increasingly realistic fears began to spread that Napoleon would cross the Channel and invade England itself. Even though the British Navy was the best in the world, its army could not hold a candle to Napoleon's massive and highly trained Grande Armée.

Though he was an incredibly intelligent military strategist, Napoleon made a few critical errors that spelled disaster for him. The first few were his ill-fated invasion of Russia, his forces' failure to capture the Iberian Peninsula, and his defeat at the Battle of Leipzig. When a European coalition managed to seize Paris as a result of his consecutive failures, he was forced to abdicate in 1814. Returning to France once again in 1815, Napoleon made more errors at the Battle of Waterloo against the British and Prussian Armies. His impetuous and irresolute behavior in addition to the waterlogged condition of the battlefield allowed the British commander, Arthur Wellesley, Duke of Wellington to take the victory. Humiliated in his defeat at the hands of the Duke of Wellington's superior strategy, Napoleon was exiled to the island of St. Helena.

After Napoleon's defeat, no other power had the economic or military mettle to challenge Great Britain's authority, and for the next one hundred years, a Pax Britannica (British Peace) settled over the world. Controlling much of the territory either directly through colonization--there was a British colony on practically every continent at this time--or indirectly through economic manipulation, Great Britain acted as the world's policeman and maintained relative global calm for a century. Skirmishes broke out to be sure, but nothing on the scale that Europe had faced over the previous centuries.

THE VICTORIAN ERA

Though managing to hold a tenuous peace abroad, at home in England there were rising tensions. The Industrial Revolution (1760-1840) had initiated a period of urban growth and the population was swelling. In the newly cramped cities, working and living conditions were abysmal, and the current small and conservative political system in England was increasingly untenable in the face of these modern pressures. In 1837, after George III's three older sons had all passed away with no surviving children, all hopes were pinned onto a young princess. Victoria, the daughter of George III's youngest son inherited the crown.

The Glorious Revolution of 1688 had formed the nation's government into a constitutional monarchy, but it was not until the Victorian Era that the British Crown adopted its modern way of operating; understanding that the monarch had limited powers, Victoria instead wielded her influence rather than her political power and became seen, especially in her later years, as a symbol for the British Empire. This clever pivot of the monarch from absolute political ruler to symbolic but influential figurehead no doubt spared the English monarchy from the bloody ends that many of their European counterparts faced from the eighteenth to the twentieth centuries. Under Victoria, the nation experienced a period of unprecedented industrial expansion. The technological developments of rail lines, steamships, and the telegraph hastened the expansion of the empire by making communication increasingly easy. Furthermore, the conservative government's tendencies towards laissez-faire economics--a hands-off approach to economic policy--allowed for great and often unchecked expansion. However, this detached way of governing often had devastating consequences for those at the lower end of the social strata. There were famines, and the most devastating example, the Irish Potato Famine or the Great Famine in the 1840s led to countless deaths as well as a massive wave of Irish emigration that changed the face of Ireland itself and many of the nations the Irish fled to.

The territorial size of the empire swelled under Victoria's rule as well. Acknowledged as the first British monarch to be the Empress of India, though India had been under the control of the British East India Company for the previous century, the Victorian Era firmly bound India to England by bringing it directly under royal control. Often referred to as the "Crown Jewel of the British Empire," India was incredibly valuable to the empire, and greatly enriched the British economy throughout the British occupation. To date, Indian people make up one of the largest proportions of immigrants into the United Kingdom and have undoubtedly contributed to the development of modern British culture. By Victoria's death in 1901, it was often said that "the sun never sets on the British Empire."

During the Pax Britannica, Europe had managed to largely avoid the bloody horrors that previous centuries had visited upon the continent. Yet as the twentieth century dawned, and Victoria's son and grandson took their turns on the English throne, trouble was brewing on the continent once more. Mounting tensions due to European imperialism, nationalism, and conflicting alliances were set to burst forth into a war unlike any the world had ever seen. Bloody, brutal, and devastating, The Great War or World War I (1914-1918) crippled Europe and stole away a generation of young men.

6

BATTLES, BLOOD, AND THE DEATH OF IMPERIALISM (1914-PRESENT DAY)

Though the assassination of Archduke Franz Ferdinand, the heir to the throne of the Austro-Hungarian Empire in 1914 is largely credited with being the spark that ignited World War I, the reality is that Europe had been slowly morphing into a volatile tinderbox for roughly twenty to thirty years before June 28, 1914. A series of "Mutual Defense Agreements" between different nations across the continent plunged the whole of Europe into horrific combat on a never-before-seen scale. The German Empire, a relatively young power that officially coalesced in 1871, was fearful of potential French and British aggression and formed the Three Emperors' League between Germany, Austria-Hungary, and Russia in 1873. This Three Emperors' League became two after Russia dropped out due to disagreements with Austria-Hungary in the Balkan States. In response to these alliances, Britain broke its period of "Splendid Isolation" and sought alliances with other European powers.

This rapid search for alliances in Europe eventually pulled the continent into two rival factions: the Triple Alliance of Germany, Austria-Hungary, and Italy and the Triple Entente of Great Britain, France, and Russia. It would only take a small act of aggression from one power for the entire continent to take up arms and rush to the defense of their allies. So, when Archduke Franz Ferdinand was shot in the Balkan State of Serbia, a longtime ally of Russia, and the Austro-Hungarian Empire declared war on Serbia, each nation gradually answered the calls of their respective allies, and the flames of World War I erupted.

By August of 1914, Germany had invaded Belgium and was marching ever closer to the French border. Not only was Great Britain allied with France through the Triple Entente, but there was also a previous agreement in place that ensured British protection of Belgium: the 1839 Treaty of London. Aware of their duties to both Belgium and France and leery of the German Army's potential to bring mainland Europe under their control, Great Britain formally entered the fray on August 4, 1914. It was a war like no other, for technology had far outstripped the military tactics of the day. In the same war that saw the first use of the modern savagery of the machine gun, heavy artillery, aerial warfare, poison gas, and tank warfare, there simultaneously existed the anachronistic, garishly colored uniforms and plumed hats of the Napoleonic Wars complete with largely useless cavalry charges on horseback. The former ways of war were resulting in massive carnage, and in response, a new form of warfare was on the horizon. As clouds of toxic chlorine gas began to roll across the battlefields, trenches were dug through Belgium and France to give the soldiers some time to put on their gas masks and offer a modicum of protection from the devastation of the machine guns.

Pulling on every resource available to it, Great Britain had summoned soldiers from every corner of the empire. So alongside a generation of young Englishmen, a generation of young Welsh, Scottish, Irish, Jamaican, Indian, Canadian, South African, Australian, New Zealander, and many other men of the empire were lost. In the end, Great Britain and its allies were successful in outlasting Germany and its allies, and the Treaty of Versailles in 1919 brought World War I to a close. And though victorious, the war shook Great Britain. Economically, it is fair to argue that the devastation of World War I played a part in the eventual dissolution of the British Empire. Morally, British subjects were forced to stare war in the face as the shellshocked young men returned home, and it became a formative event for many of the twentieth century's most enduring literary voices, like C.S. Lewis, J.R.R. Tolkien, T.S. Eliot, among others. The joy of a British victory combined with the dark traumas of war forged large pieces of the modern British identity, sweeping away the elegant and stratified society of the Victorian and Edwardian Eras and giving way to a more democratic social world. The first early inklings of the modern welfare system in England, first seen at the beginning of the twentieth century, gained more traction and support during the postwar era. Even the Royal Family, in the wake of virulent anti-German sentiment, changed their formal surname from Saxe-Coburg and Gotha--which it had been since Victoria's son King George V--to the more palatable British name of Windsor.

In the wake of the Great War, and as the twentieth century continued to speed forward, Great Britain was unable to maintain its vast empire, due to a mix of economic strain and nationalist sentiments growing within their colonies. The strain might have simply destroyed other empires and led to the ruin of the mother nation. But in true British fashion, it was a matter of simply pivoting away from an imperial model to one more palatable for the modern age. Since the late 1800s, Great Britain had maintained some control over former colonies that had gained a modicum of independence by classifying them as "Dominions." By 1926, these Dominions had all agreed to swear allegiance to the king or queen of Great Britain, but asserted their rights as equal members within the British Empire; the United Kingdom did not rule over them. This agreement forged the new status of the British Empire moving into the twentieth and twenty-first centuries: the British Commonwealth. As time passed, more colonies became independent states wishing to remain with the Commonwealth but not too keen to swear allegiance to the monarch of Great Britain. To rectify this, the 1949 Commonwealth Prime Ministers Meeting issued the London Declaration which allowed republics and other outside countries to retain or gain membership in the Commonwealth. To date, there are fifty-four countries in the Commonwealth and membership is completely voluntary. By allowing an empire to seamlessly melt into a commonwealth, England has managed to keep a larger presence and influence across the globe than other countries like Spain and France whose empires simply collapsed alongside the usefulness of imperialism in the nineteenth and twentieth centuries.

During the economic hardship felt across the globe in the 1930s, Germany, now under Hitler, was rising in militaristic might once more. When Germany invaded Poland in 1939, Great Britain responded by once again, declaring war as Europe was hurled headfirst into another vicious global conflict, a mere twenty-one years since the last one had ended. Though sending troops to the continent once again, there was something uniquely new and horrifying for this island nation. Historically protected from large-scale invasions from mainland Europe thanks to the English Channel, the rise of aerial combat in the First World War had shattered the illusion of safety for the English people. Zeppelins had attacked from above in World War I, but these were slow-moving, unwieldy, highly flammable, and easily shot down. By World War II, the German Luftwaffe and the British Royal Air Force (RAF) were powerful fighting forces, and the first fully aerial battle, the Battle of Britain, was fought in the skies over Europe in 1940. Though the skill of the RAF undoubtedly kept the Nazi forces at bay and successfully kept them from furthering their designs on Great Britain, the Germans were not so easily deterred. A German bombing campaign known as the Blitz (1940-41) destroyed large swaths of British cities and took countless civilian lives, leading to a collective national trauma. The barbarity experienced by both the military and by civilians in both World Wars forged a resilient English identity that paired well with a powerful nationalistic sentiment that had begun to grow in the nineteenth century. As the Prime Minister of the time, Winston Churchill said in his rousing speech to the House of Commons in the summer of 1940, "Let us, therefore, brace ourselves to our duties, and so bear ourselves that if the British Empire and its Commonwealth last for a thousand years, men will still say, 'This was their finest hour.'" (Churchill, 1940)

After the war, the destruction of the continent's infrastructure and the widespread loss of life led to economic calamity. Great Britain could no longer claim to be the world's preeminent power; after all, the United States, a former colony of the empire, and geographically isolated from the devastation in Europe was in its ascendancy. Political power in Parliament swung away from Churchill's Conservative Party to the more liberal Labour Party, and the modern welfare state was fully established, including the founding of the publicly funded National Health Service (NHS).

After years of tension, both Ireland and India left the Empire and were controversially partitioned on their way out the door. India was split into India and Pakistan, while Ireland was divided into the independent Republic of Ireland and Northern Ireland, which remained in the United Kingdom. Issues with Ireland would continue for thirty years during the Troubles (1968-1998), a period of social unrest and violence resulting from nationalistic Irish organizations like the Irish Republican Army (IRA) and Sinn Féin clashing with British and pro-British forces. Great Britain also joined the United Nations (UN) and the European Economic Community (EEC), which would later morph into the European Union.

Throughout the Cold War, the United Kingdom maintained close economic and military ties with the United States and its historic allies on the European continent, joining the North Atlantic Treaty Organization (NATO) in response to the rising threat from the Soviet Bloc to the east. In 1979, the Conservative Party came back into power with the election of Margaret Thatcher, the first female Prime Minister. Much like "Reaganism" in the United States, "Thatcherism" in the United Kingdom was characterized by its unwavering beliefs in a small state government and a free market that was born out through increased privatization and deregulation. Though she managed to increase efficiency in some markets through increased competition and homeownership went up under her tenure, her policies also caused mass unemployment and recessions. Depending on who is speaking, she is either revered or despised.

Despite meddling in affairs all over the world for the better part of four centuries, England has remained fiercely averse to any nation, entity, or organization disturbing its sovereignty. When the euro was introduced in 1999 as the currency for the European Union, England refused, insisting on maintaining the pound sterling. Perhaps it is the result of being an island country or perhaps it is the nation's history as a powerful player on the world's stage, but England has bristled at any further assertion of power from the European Union, and in June of 2016, Great Britain narrowly voted to leave the EU ("Brexit"). With Brexit officially occurring in January of 2020, there have been sentiments of unrest throughout the United Kingdom. In Scotland and Northern Ireland, a higher percentage of the population wished to remain within the European Union, while the majority voted to leave in England. Whispers that Brexit may fracture the United Kingdom are not mere speculation; Scotland's National Party, the current majority party in Scotland, is interested in pushing a second independence referendum. This would potentially undo the political union between Scotland and England that has officially been in place since 1707. To England's west, unrest in Northern Ireland, similar to the days of the Troubles in the late twentieth century, is on the rise.

So England, like so many other nations in the twenty-first century, is at another crossroads. The demographics of the nation are changing, as are the needs of its people. In fact, many of the immigrants in England come from the United Kingdom's former colonies, and just as the English shaped their native country's culture and history, they now have a hand in the formation of the future of the United Kingdom. So its government, somehow simultaneously rigid and malleable over the years, will have to shift with the changing tides of the twenty-first century. Where the future will find England is anyone's guess. But if history is to be believed, it will continue, like its language, ever-growing, ever-changing, and still somehow quintessentially English. George Orwell put it best, *"England will still be England, an everlasting animal stretching into the future and the past, and, like all living things, having the power to change out of recognition and yet remain the same."* (Orwell, 1941, p. 279).

PRAISE FOR DOMINIC HAYNES

I hope you enjoyed this book. If you did, I'd appreciate it if you left a review on Amazon. Your reviews are the lifeblood of my business and I incorporate the feedback into future books.

To leave a review, go to:
Amazon.com/review/create-review?
&asin=B097LWPR77
Or scan with your camera:

OTHER BOOKS BY DOMINIC HAYNES

(AVAILABLE ON AMAZON & AUDIBLE)

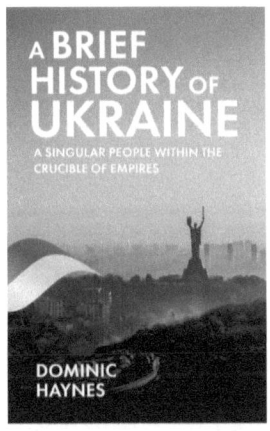

A Brief History of Ukraine: A Singular People Within the Crucible of Empires

A Brief History of Canada: How the Clash of French, British and Native Empires Forged a Unique Identity

A Brief History of America: Contradictions & Divisions in the United States from the Revolutionary Era to the Present Day

REFERENCES

Borman, T. (2017). *The Private Lives of the Tudors*. Grove Press.

Bovey, A. (2015, April 30). *Peasants and their role in rural life*. British Library. https://www.bl.uk/the-middle-ages/articles/peasants-and-their-role-in-rural-life

Brain, J. (n.d.). *The Field of the Cloth of Gold*. Historic UK. https://www.historic-uk.com/HistoryUK/HistoryofEngland/Field-of-The-Cloth-Of-Gold/

British Broadcasting Corporation/BBC News. (2016, June 23). *EU Referendum Results*. British Broadcasting Corporation/BBC. https://www.bbc.com/news/politics/eu_referendum/results

Churchill, W. (1940, June 18). *Their Finest Hour* [Text]. Churchill. https://winstonchurchill.org/resources/speeches/1940-the-finest-hour/their-finest-hour/

Clark, G., Elliott, S., Locke, B. (Producers) & Clark, G., Elliott, S. (Directors). (2013). *Henry VII: Winter King* [Video file]. Retrieved from https://www.youtube.com/watch?v=8wXTB52oUYE

Crowther, D. (Host). (2010-present). *The History of England* [Audio podcast]. https://thehistoryofengland.co.uk/

Editors, T. (n.d.). *Anglo-Saxons: a brief history*. Historical Association. https://www.history.org.uk/primary/resource/3865/anglo-saxons-a-brief-history

Editor, T. (n.d). *An Introduction to Victorian England (1837-1901)*. English Heritage. https://www.english-heritage.org.uk/learn/story-of-england/victorian/

Editor, T. (2011, January 13). *The Vikings in Britain: a brief history*. Historical Association. https://www.history.org.uk/primary/resource/3867/the-vikings-in-britain-a-brief-history

Editors, T. (2020, July 8). *Battle of Britain*. History. https://www.history.com/topics/world-war-ii/battle-of-britain-1

Editors, T. (2018, August 21). *Hadrian's Wall*. History. https://www.history.com/topics/ancient-rome/hadrians-wall

Editors, T. (2018, August 21). *Hundred Years' War*. History. https://www.history.com/topics/middle-ages/hundred-years-war

Editors, T. (2019, December 2). *Royal Succession*. History. https://www.history.com/topics/british-history/royal-succession

Editors, T. (2020, June 3). *Wars of the Roses*. History. https://www.history.com/topics/british-history/wars-of-the-roses#section_11

Editors, T. (2019, October 24). *Who Were Celts*. History. https://www.history.com/topics/ancient-history/celts

Gold, D. (Executive Producer). (2016). *Britain's Bloody Crown* [TV Series]. Channel 5 Productions.

Harrison, J. (n.d.). *Who were the Anglo-Saxons?*. British Library. https://www.bl.uk/anglo-saxons/articles/who-were-the-anglo-saxons

Hickey, P., Saville, L., Sparks, E. (Executive Producers). (2018). *The Stuarts: A Bloody Reign* [TV Series]. 3DD Productions.

Hirst, M. (2021, April 14). *NI Riots: What is behind the violence in Northern Ireland?*. British Broadcasting Corporation/BBC. https://www.bbc.com/news/uk-northern-ireland-56664378

Hudson, A. (n.d.). *How was the kingdom of England formed?*. British Library. https://www.bl.uk/anglo-saxons/articles/how-was-the-kingdom-of-england-formed

Hudson, J. (2011, February 17). *What Did the Normans Do for Us?*. The British Broadcasting Company/BBC. http://www.bbc.co.uk/history/british/normans/hudson_norman_01.shtml

Johnson, B. (n.d.). *The Romans in England*. Historic UK. https://www.historic-uk.com/HistoryUK/HistoryofEngland/The-Romans-in-England

Johnson, B. (2012). *Timeline of Events AD 700-2012*. Historic UK. https://www.historic-uk.com/HistoryUK/HistoryofBritain/Timeline-of-Events-AD-700-2012/

Keegan, J. (1998). *The First World War*. Vintage Books.

Kiger, P. J. (2021, April 7). *8 Events that Led to World War I*. History. https://www.history.com/news/world-war-i-causes

Lyons, B. (Director). (1999, June 29). Blood Red Roses (Season 1, Episode 1) [TV Series Episode]. In B. Lyons (Executive Producer), *Secrets of the Dead*. Channel Four Television Corporation.

Mather, R. (2014, May 15). *The impact of the Napoleonic Wars in Britain*. British Library. https://www.bl.uk/romantics-and-victorians/articles/the-impact-of-the-napoleonic-wars-in-britain

Nelson, J. (2016, January 5). *The death of Edward the Confessor and the conflicting claims to the English Crown*. Gov.UK. https://history.blog.gov.uk/2016/01/05/the-death-of-edward-the-confessor-and-the-conflicting-claims-to-the-english-crown/

Orwell, G. (1981). England Your England. *A Collection of Essays* (1st ed., pp. 252-279). Harcourt.

Parliament of the United Kingdom (n.d.). *Anglo-Saxon origins*. UK Parliament. https://www.parliament.uk/about/living-heritage/evolutionofparliament/originsofparliament/birthofparliament/overview/origins/

Poole, M. (Executive Producers). (2014). *The First Georgians: The German Kings Who Made Britain* [TV Series]. British Broadcasting Company/BBC.

Scoones, E. (Director). (2013, April 22). Happy Families: Hanoverians to Windsors (Season 1, Episode 3) [TV Series Episode]. In E. Hindley (Executive Producers). *Fit to Rule: How Royal Illness Changed History*. British Broadcasting Company/BBC.

The British Commonwealth. (n.d.). *Our History*. The Commonwealth. https://thecommonwealth.org/about-us/history

The British Library (n.d.). *The True Law of Free Monarchies by James VI and I*. British Library.https://www.bl.uk/collection-items/the-true-law-of-free-monarchies-by-king-james-vi-and-i

The National Archives. (n.d.). *God blew and they were scattered*. The National Archives. https://www.nationalarchives.gov.uk/education/resources/god-blew-they-were-scattered/

The National Archives (n.d.). *Jacobite Timeline: Timeline of Key Events During the Jacobite Rebellions*. The National Archives. https://nationalarchives.gov.uk/documents/education/timeline-final.pdf

The National Archives. (n.d.). *The Great War 1914 to 1918*. The National

Archives. https://www.nationalarchives.gov.uk/education/greatwar/g2/backgroundcs1.htm

The Royal Family (n.d.). *Alfred 'The Great'* (r. 871-899). The Royal Family. https://www.royal.uk/alfred-great-r-871-899

The Royal Family (n.d.). *Elizabeth I* (r. 1558-1603). The Royal Family. https://www.royal.uk/elizabeth-i

The Royal Family (n.d.). *George I* (r. 1714-1727). The Royal Family. https://www.royal.uk/george-i

The Royal Family (n.d.). *Henry I 'Beauclerc'* (r. 1100-1135). The Royal Family. https://www.royal.uk/henry-i

The Royal Family (n.d.). *The Plantagenets*. The Royal Family. https://www.royal.uk/plantagenets

The Royal Family. (n.d.). *Victoria* (r. 1837-1901). The Royal Family. https://www.royal.uk/queen-victoria

Trueman, C. N. (2015, March 17). *James and Parliament*. History Learning Site. https://www.historylearningsite.co.uk/stuart-england/james-and-parliament/

www.ingramcontent.com/pod-product-compliance
Lightning Source LLC
Chambersburg PA
CBHW030311100526
44590CB00012B/594